Sara Swan Miller

Salamanders

Secret, Silent Lives

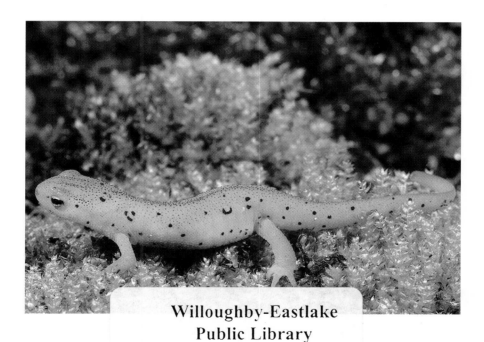

Willoughby-Eastlake
Public Library

Franklin Watts - A Division of Grolier Publishing
New York • London • Hong Kong • Sydney • Danbury, Connecticut

For Ann Guenther

Photographs ©: Animals Animals: 5 bottom right (John Gerlach), 1, 34, 35 (Breck P. Kent), 5 top right, 5 top left, 7, 15, 17 (Zig Leszczynski), 37 (Fred Whitehead); Photo Researchers: 6 (John M. Burnley), cover, 21 (Suzanne L. & Joseph T. Collins), 23 (Jack Dermid), 29, 31 (Phil A. Dotson), 32, 33, 39 (Tom McHugh); Superstock, Inc. 5 bottom left, 25; Tony Stone Images: 40 (Frank Siteman); Visuals Unlimited: 42 (Bill Banaszewski), 13, 19 (Rob Simpson), 27 (Rob & Ann Simpson), 43 (L. S. Stepanowicz), 41 (Gustav W. Verderber).

Illustrations by Jose Gonzales and Steve Savage

Visit Franklin Watts on the Internet at:
http://publishing.grolier.com

Library of Congress Cataloging-in-Publication Data

Miller, Sara Swan.
Salamanders: secret, silent lives / Sara Swan Miller.
        p. cm. — (Animals in order)
    Includes bibliographical references and index.
    Summary: An introduction to salamanders that includes descriptions of fourteen species and recommendations for finding, identifying, and observing them.
    ISBN 0-531-11568-2 (lib. bdg.)   0-531-16402-0 (pbk.)
    1. Salamanders—Juvenile literature. [1. Salamanders.] I. Title. II. Series.
QL668.C2M47   1999
597.8′5—dc21
                                                    98-5200
                                                    CIP
                                                    AC

© 1999 Franklin Watts, A Division of Grolier Publishing
All rights reserved. Published simultaneously in Canada.
Printed in the United States of America.
1 2 3 4 5 6 7 8 9 10 R 08 07 06 05 04 03 02 01 00 99

Contents

How Do You Know
It's a Salamander?

Have you ever found a small animal with four legs and a tail hiding under a rock? Did you say, "Look! A lizard!"? Chances are, that animal wasn't a lizard. It was probably a salamander. At first glance, salamanders and lizards look a lot alike. They are about the same shape, and they hold their bodies pretty much the same way.

If you studied these animals closely, you would see that they are really very different. They live in different *habitats*. Salamanders live in cool, moist places. If a salamander gets too hot or dries out, it will die. Lizards prefer dry, hot places. They are most often found in deserts or tropical regions of the world.

Salamanders and lizards are different in other ways, too. A salamander's body is covered with slippery skin, while a lizard's skin is covered with tough scales. No salamander has more than four toes on its front feet, but most lizards have five. Lizards have claws on their feet, but most salamanders do not.

On the next page are two salamanders and two lizards. Can you see some of the ways they are different from one another?

Spotted salamander

Leopard lizard

Red-backed salamander

Side-blotched lizard

Traits of a Salamander

Even though salamanders and lizards look similar, they are not closely related. Lizards are *reptiles*. They are closely related to turtles, snakes, and crocodiles. Salamanders are not reptiles. They belong to a group of animals called *amphibians*. Frogs and toads are also amphibians.

All salamanders are *carnivores* that eat insects, worms, and other small animals. They may even eat each other! Salamanders depend on their eyes and on their good sense of smell to find *prey*. Salamanders have simple ears. They cannot hear the way we do, but they can pick up vibrations with their front legs. These vibrations travel through muscle to a bone in their head. They don't have vocal cords, either, so most salamanders are completely silent.

A marbled salamander

6

Because salamander eggs have no shells, they must be laid in water or in moist places on land. The *larvae* that hatch from these eggs look a lot like tadpoles. You can tell the difference by looking at the gills. Tadpoles have two gills on each side of their head, while salamander larvae have three. Some kinds of salamanders don't lay eggs. Instead, the eggs hatch inside the mother, and the young are born ready to creep about on land.

Salamanders have *glands* under their skin that produce *mucus* to keep them moist and help them slip through the water. Other glands make poisons that help keep salamanders safe from *predators*. A salamander's bright colors warn enemies that it is poisonous. They are like a big sign that says, "Don't eat me! I taste bad!"

Eggs of a four-toed salamander

7

The Order of Living Things

A tiger has more in common with a house cat than with a daisy. A true bug is more like a butterfly than a jellyfish. Scientists arrange living things into groups based on how they look and how they act. A tiger and a house cat belong to the same group, but a daisy belongs to a different group.

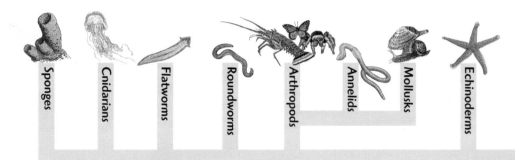

Sponges | Cnidarians | Flatworms | Roundworms | Arthropods | Annelids | Mollusks | Echinoderms

Animals

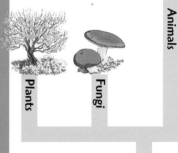

Plants | Fungi

Protists

Monerans

All living things can be placed in one of five groups called *kingdoms*: the plant kingdom, the animal kingdom, the fungus kingdom, the moneran kingdom, or the protist kingdom. You can probably name many of the creatures in the plant and animal kingdoms. The fungus kingdom includes mushrooms, yeasts, and molds. The moneran and protist kingdoms contain thousands of living things that are too small to see without a microscope.

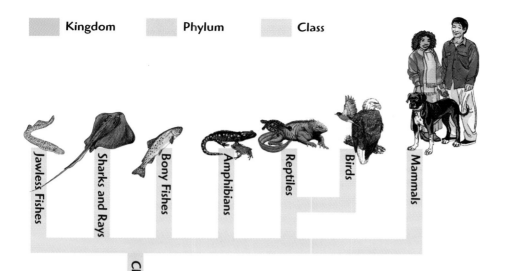

Kingdom   Phylum   Class

Jawless Fishes

Sharks and Rays

Bony Fishes

Amphibians

Reptiles

Birds

Mammals

Chordates

Because there are millions and millions of living things on Earth, some of the members of one kingdom may not seem all that similar. The animal kingdom includes creatures as different as tarantulas and trout, jellyfish and jaguars, salamanders and sparrows, elephants and earthworms.

To show that an elephant is more like a jaguar than an earthworm, scientists further separate the creatures in each kingdom into more specific groups. The animal kingdom can be divided into nine *phyla*. Humans belong to the chordate phylum. Almost all chordates have a backbone.

Each phylum can be subdivided into many *classes*. Humans, mice, and elephants all belong to the *mammal* class. Each class can be further divided into *orders*; orders into *families*, families into *genera*, and genera into *species*. All the members of a species are very similar.

9

How Salamanders Fit In

You can probably guess that salamanders belong to the animal kingdom. They have much more in common with swordfish and snakes than with maple trees and morning glories.

Salamanders belong to the chordate phylum. Almost all chordates have a backbone and a skeleton. Can you think of other chordates? Examples include elephants, mice, turtles, frogs, birds, fish, and whales.

All amphibians belong to the same class. There are three different orders of amphibians. Salamanders make up one of these orders. Frogs and toads belong to a separate order of amphibians. The third kind of amphibian is called a caecilian. Because caecilians have no legs, they look like a cross between a snake and an earthworm.

Salamanders can be divided into a number of different families and genera. These groups can be broken down into hundreds of species. You will learn more about fourteen species of salamanders in this book.

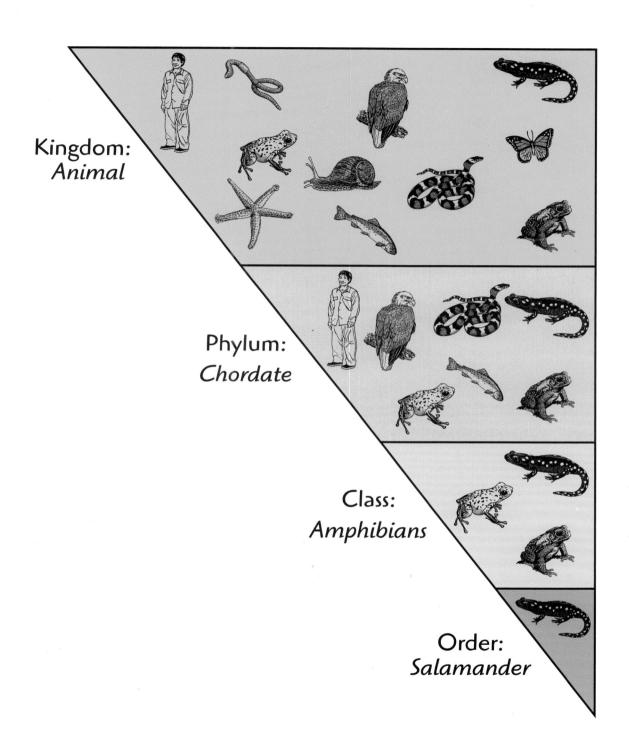

Kingdom:
Animal

Phylum:
Chordate

Class:
Amphibians

Order:
Salamander

Newts

FAMILY: Salamandridae

COMMON EXAMPLE: Eastern newt

GENUS AND SPECIES: *Notophthalmus viridescens*

SIZE: 2 5/8 to 5 1/2 inches (6.5 to 14 cm)

Have you ever come across a small, bright-orange salamander in the woods? You were probably looking at a young eastern newt. At this stage of its life, the newt is called a "red *eft*." Did you wonder why this delicate little creature wasn't hiding safely under the leaves? Red efts don't need to hide from enemies because their skin is coated with poison. No one wants a taste of that!

In early spring, eastern newts, also called red-spotted newts, hatch from eggs laid in a pond. They begin life as tiny brownish larvae. As they dart around the pond in search of food, the larvae breathe through gills. By fall, the newts are larger and their skin is bright orange. They have lost their gills and grown lungs, so they are ready to crawl out of the water and journey into the woods.

Red efts live in the woods for 1 to 3 years. They spend their time gobbling up insects and worms. When they are fully grown newts, they return to the pond where they were born. The newts pair up and mate, and then the females lay eggs. Both males and females lose their bright coloring. Their backs turn olive green and their bellies turn yellow. Their bodies are sprinkled with red and black dots.

For the rest of their lives, the eastern newts live in the pond where they were born. They spend their days resting just under the water's surface. When they get hungry, they eat worms, water insects, small shrimp and snails, frog eggs, fish eggs, and tadpoles.

Spotted Salamanders

FAMILY: *Ambystomidae*
COMMON NAME: Spotted salamander
GENUS AND SPECIES: *Ambystoma maculatum*
SIZE: 6 to 9 3/4 inches (15 to 25 cm)

The first rains of spring have been falling all day, melting the winter snow. Night comes, and the rain is still falling. Suddenly, the ground comes alive with salamanders! Hundreds of the spotted creatures trek through the melting snow.

The squirming salamanders are heading for the woodland pool where they were born. The males get there first and mill about in large groups until the females arrive. Then the mating dance begins!

It starts slowly. A group of males circle around a female, nosing and nudging her. Soon, the pace picks up, and the mating dance turns into a frenzy. Everywhere salamanders are slipping over and under each other, circling and chasing, until the water boils!

Finally, the salamanders mate and everything settles down. Two or 3 days later, the females lay one or two clumps of jellylike eggs in the water. The eggs stick to the twigs and stems of water plants. By the time the larvae hatch, the adult salamanders are long gone.

Adult spotted salamanders spend most of their lives underground, quietly feeding on insects, worms, and grubs. But when the first spring rains begin to fall, they appear out of nowhere and begin their journey to the pool where they were born.

Tiger Salamanders

FAMILY: Ambystomidae
COMMON EXAMPLE: Eastern tiger salamander
GENUS AND SPECIES: *Ambystoma tigrinum*
SIZE: 6 to 13 3/8 inches (15 to 40 cm)

Tiger salamanders are the largest land-living salamanders in the world. They look a lot like spotted salamanders and act like them, too. Both species are in the same family—the mole salamanders.

It's easy to guess how mole salamanders got their name. Most of them live underground in the *burrows* of crayfish or small mammals. They spend most of their time gobbling up earthworms and large insects. Sometimes, tiger salamanders eat small frogs or mice. They come to the surface only on rainy nights.

When the first spring rains fall, tiger salamanders crawl out of their burrows and begin the long trek to the pond where they were born. Sometimes they travel more than 1 mile (1.6 km)!

How do they find their way back? No one knows. A part of their brain may act like a compass that helps them return to their home pond. It is also possible that they recognize landmarks they passed when they traveled away from their pond the year before. Most scientists think that their excellent sense of smell helps them find the pond. It's truly amazing that these small, slow-moving creatures can make a beeline to their home pond when the spring rain calls out "mating time!"

17

Dusky Salamanders

FAMILY: Plethodontidae
COMMON EXAMPLE: Northern dusky
  salamander
GENUS AND SPECIES: *Desmognathus fuscus*
SIZE: 2 1/2 to 5 1/2 inches (6.5 to 14 cm)

The dusky salamander belongs to a big family—the lungless salamanders. Even though this salamander has no lungs, it spends most of its life on land. How does it breathe? As long as it stays moist, the dusky salamander can get plenty of oxygen through its skin and the lining of its mouth.

Duskies hide out under wet leaves during the day. They seem to like company. Large groups of these salamanders often pile on top of one another in their hiding place. At night, the salamanders come out to hunt for worms, slugs, and small soft-bodied insects. Beware, salamanders! There are plenty of small snakes and frogs hunting for you!

Many kinds of salamanders do not take care of their eggs once they are laid. Dusky salamanders are different. After the female lays her eggs, she wraps herself around them until they hatch. Then the larvae follow trickles of water to a nearby stream, and spend the fall and winter in the water. By spring, they are full grown and can join the adults on land.

The dusky salamander has a good trick for escaping from predators. If it is scared, it will suddenly jump up in the air and land several inches away. It's hard to imagine how this stumpy-legged creature can leap at all. Salamanders are full of surprises!

Cave Salamanders

FAMILY: Plethodontidae
COMMON EXAMPLE: Cave salamander
GENUS AND SPECIES: *Eurycea lucifuga*
SIZE: 4 7/8 to 7 1/8 inches (12.5 to 18 cm)

As you might guess, cave salamanders like to hide out in caves. But not just any old cave will do. The only place you will find them is in the limestone caves of Virginia and nearby states.

No salamander likes water with high levels of acid in it, but cave salamanders are especially sensitive to acid. Like other lungless salamanders, cave salamanders have a groove running from their nose down to their upper lip. This is a special organ that helps them sense different chemicals in the water. If the water is acidic, they can tell right away. A cave is a perfect home for this salamander because limestone is not acidic, so the water running through the cave has very little acid in it.

When the larvae of cave salamanders hatch in the water, they are only 3/8 inch (1 cm) long. Because the water inside a cave is cold, very few animals live in it. There isn't much for the young salamanders to eat, so they grow very slowly. It takes a whole year for them to grow to 2 inches (5 cm) long. When the salamanders are big enough, they lose their gills and crawl out to find better hunting grounds.

You may find them around the entrance to a cave, where the light is dim and the air is moist. They clamber all over the walls, poking their noses into cracks in search of insects to eat. They can even hang from their tails, like tiny monkeys!

Four-toed Salamanders

FAMILY: Plethodontidae
COMMON NAME: Four-toed salamander
GENUS AND SPECIES: *Hemidactilium scutatum*
SIZE: 2 to 4 inches (5 to 10 cm)

A four-toed salamander creeps slowly along the forest floor, hunting for tasty insects. Suddenly, a big crow lands next to the salamander and grabs its tail. Is the salamander about to be eaten?

Not at all! This salamander has an amazing trick. Its tail breaks off from its body and lies wriggling on the ground. While the crow jabs at the tail, the salamander dives to safety under the leaves. It won't be anybody's lunch today!

The tail of a four-toed salamander has a built-in breaking point. It pops off cleanly when an enemy snatches it. Soon, a new tail will grow, and the salamander will be able to survive another attack the same way.

Most salamanders have five toes on their hind feet, but this salamander has only four. That's how it got its name!

It isn't easy to spot four-toed salamanders. You have to know just where to look. The adults live under stones and leaf litter in *hardwood forests* near a *bog*. The bog is important at mating time. Female salamanders attach their eggs, one at a time, to *sphagnum*—a type of moss that grows close to the water. Like female dusky salamanders, four-toed females guard their eggs until they hatch. Then the tiny larvae slip into the bog and get to work gobbling up even smaller animals.

Red-backed Salamanders

FAMILY: Plethodontidae
COMMON NAME: Red-backed salamander
GENUS AND SPECIES: *Plethodon cinereus*
SIZE: 2 1/2 to 5 inches (6.5 to 13 cm)

A red-backed salamander doesn't always live up to its name. Sometimes it has a gray stripe on its back instead of a red one. If you look under stones and logs in a hardwood forest, you may find some of these salamanders. How many can you find? In a healthy forest, there may be as many as 16,000 in 1 acre (0.4 hectare)!

Finding a lot of red-backed salamanders in a woodland is a good sign. These salamanders can't live in soils with high levels of acid. Most trees and shrubs don't grow well in acid soils, either. If you find red-backed salamanders, you know that the soil is just right.

These salamanders actually help to make the soil even healthier. They eat insects and other small animals that feed on fallen leaves and other decaying plant matter. As a result, the salamander's droppings are full of materials that help trees and shrubs to grow.

In the summer, female red-backs lay eggs. They coil around their eggs to protect them from enemies. The young red-backs go through their larval stage while they are still inside the eggs. When they hatch, they look like tiny adults. They are less than 1 inch (2.5 cm) long, but they are ready to hunt on their own.

24

Slimy Salamanders
FAMILY: Plethodontidae
COMMON NAME: Slimy salamander
GENUS AND SPECIES: *Plethodon glutinosus*
SIZE: 4 1/2 to 8 1/8 inches (11.5 to 20.5 cm)

If you ever pick up a slimy salamander, you'll understand how it got its name. It's covered from head to tail with a slimy covering that sticks to your hands like glue. It seems almost impossible to wash off!

Its sticky slime helps this salamander to protect itself from enemies. If a fox or a bird tries to eat a slimy salamander, it will drop the salamander right away. Who wants to get a mouthful of glue?

Of course, before predators can attack a slimy salamander, they have to be able to see it. Most of the time, that isn't easy. Its glossy black skin is speckled with white spots, so it looks like a stick covered with fungus.

The slimy salamander lives its whole life on land. The female lays her eggs under rocks or logs and guards them until they hatch. Like many other lungless salamanders, the young go through their larval stage inside the eggs. They look like miniature versions of their parents when they hatch.

Even though slimy salamanders are one of the largest and most widespread of the lungless salamanders, you may never see one. They hide under stones or rotting logs during the day. On rainy evenings, they come out of hiding and hunt for insects on the forest floor.

Arboreal Salamanders

FAMILY: Plethodontidae
COMMON NAME: Arboreal salamander
GENUS AND SPECIES: *Aneides lugubris*
SIZE: 4 1/4 to 7 1/4 inches (11 to 18.5 cm)

What's that salamander doing? It's hanging from a tree! Arboreal salamanders are the champion climbers of the salamander world. In fact, one was found in a mouse's nest 60 feet (18 m) up a tree!

The word "arboreal" means "living in trees." It's a good name for these salamanders because that's where many arboreals spend most of their time. Other arboreal salamanders live on the ground in tree stumps or in rock walls. Still others live underground in basements, mine shafts, or rodent burrows.

Arboreal salamanders eat small animals, and may also feed on fungus. Besides the tiny spiny teeth that all salamanders have, arboreal salamanders have large teeth in their lower jaw. Scientists think they use these special teeth to scrape fungus off hard surfaces.

Arboreal salamanders seem to like company. More than thirty of them have been found packed together in a tree hole. While other lungless salamanders breathe through their skin, arboreal salamanders also breathe through their toes!

When they're scared, arboreal salamanders squeak like mice. Yet they have no lungs or vocal cords. To make sound, they force air through their jaws and nostrils with their throat muscles. How amazing!

Hellbenders

FAMILY: Cryptobranchidae
COMMON NAME: Hellbender
GENUS AND SPECIES: *Cryptobranchus alleganiensis*
SIZE: 12 to 29 1/8 inches (30.5 to 74 cm)

Some people think that the hellbender looks more like a bad dream than a living thing! This fleshy salamander has a flattened head and deeply wrinkled, very slimy skin that looks as though it is several sizes too large for its body.

When the hellbender is out of water, it looks like a flat blob of jelly. But this salamander is rarely on land. It spends most of its life in fast-moving rivers where there is a lot of oxygen mixed in with the water. The hellbender has no lungs or gills, so it breathes entirely through its skin. The salamander's wrinkly skin absorbs plenty of oxygen and helps it breathe better.

During the day, hellbenders hide under rocks or fallen trees in the river. At night, they wriggle out and prowl along the riverbed, searching for worms, crayfish, and other small creatures.

A female hellbender lays as many as 2,000 eggs at a time. You might find a long string of these eggs stuck to stones underwater. The male is supposed to guard the eggs until they hatch, but if he gets hungry, he may eat some of them. It's a good thing the female lays so many!

Sometimes, people who are fishing catch hellbenders by mistake. These salamanders are so scary looking that people often cut their fishing lines rather than handle a hellbender. They think the salamanders are poisonous, but they aren't. Hellbenders look hideous, but they won't poison anybody.

Sirens

FAMILY: Sirenidae

COMMON EXAMPLE: Greater siren

GENUS AND SPECIES: *Siren lacertina*

SIZE: 19 3/4 to 38 1/2 inches (50 to 98 cm)

Have you ever seen a snake lurking in the weeds at the edge of a pond? If you looked more closely, you might have noticed that the slippery creature had tiny front legs. If it also had big, yellow, feathery gills, you were looking at a greater siren—not a snake.

Sirens are named after the legendary sea creatures who supposedly sang to sailors. These beautiful mermaids were said to have the head and upper body of a woman and the tail of a fish. The type of salamanders called greater sirens are not especially beautiful, and they don't sing. The best they can do is make a small yelping or whistling sound.

But, like the mythical sirens, they do live in water. They are found in shallow rivers choked with weeds. The weeds keep them safe from predators while they dine on crayfish and snails. On rainy nights, greater sirens sometimes crawl out of the water and slither a little way on land.

What happens if their pond dries up? The salamanders dig their way into the mud and make a cocoon of mucus around themselves. Only their snout sticks out. Their heart rate slows way down, and they sleep for weeks or months. They do not come out until heavy rains fill their pond with water.

A siren is usually safe as long as it stays hidden in weeds, but it has one important enemy. Rainbow snakes also lurk in the weeds around ponds hoping to see a greater siren slither by.

Mudpuppies

FAMILY: Proteidae
COMMON NAME: Mudpuppy
GENUS AND SPECIES: *Necturus maculosus*
SIZE: 8 to 17 inches (20 to 43 cm)

Some people call them "mudpuppies" and others call them "waterdogs," but these salamanders don't look like dogs or puppies. So, where do these strange names come from? Many years ago someone said that these salamanders bark like dogs. No one else had ever heard mudpuppies bark, but they believed the story anyway. Today, we know that mudpuppies don't make any sound at all.

A mudpuppy never leaves the water. If it did, it would suffocate. It breathes through bushy red gills its whole life—even as an adult. You can get an idea of how cold a pond is by looking at a mudpuppy's gills. If the water is cold and full of oxygen, its gills are smaller. But in warm, stagnant water a mudpuppy needs large gills to get enough oxygen.

34

You may have a hard time finding one of these salamanders. They spend their days hiding on the weedy bottom of lakes or ponds. At night, they come out and swim slowly as they hunt for fish, water insects, and crayfish.

In spring, female mudpuppies lay small, yellow, globe-shaped eggs on the undersides of submerged rocks or logs. The mother stays close to her eggs and guards them from enemies.

Amphiumas

FAMILY: Amphiumidae
COMMON EXAMPLE: Two-toed amphiuma
GENUS AND SPECIES: *Amphiuma means*
SIZE: 18 to 45 3/4 inches (46 to 116 cm)

Believe it or not, the two-toed amphiuma is sometimes called a "Congo eel." What a confusing name! These salamanders don't live in the Congo, and they certainly aren't eels. Eels are a kind of fish.

A two-toed amphiuma looks a lot like an eel, though. It has tiny, useless legs, and it wriggles through the water. Like an eel, the amphiuma's gills are inside its head, and it has no eyelids or tongue.

This salamander stays underwater most of the time. During the day, it burrows into the bottom mud and hides from enemies. At night, the two-toed amphiuma hunts for crayfish and snails. If it's rainy, the salamander may come out onto land and slither along the muddy bank. But when the sun rises, the amphiuma goes home to its burrow.

A female amphiuma lays her eggs in long strings under a stone or log on the muddy riverbank. She coils around the eggs and guards them until they hatch 5 months later. That's a long time to stay in one place! When the tiny larvae hatch, they wait for a good rain, then quickly slither down to the river.

Don't ever try to pick up a Congo eel! Unlike most salamanders, it is quick to defend itself. Its sharp teeth are very small, but they can give you a big, painful bite!

Giant Salamanders
FAMILY: Cryptobranchidae
EXAMPLE: Chinese giant salamander
GENUS AND SPECIES: *Andreas davidianus*
SIZE: 36 to 71 inches (91 to 180 cm)

This salamander really is a giant! From its nose to its tail, it's as long as a man is tall! It looks strange, too—like something out of a science-fiction movie. Its head is large and flat, and its legs are short and stocky. A ridge of very wrinkled skin runs down the sides of its head and body. Like the hellbender, the Chinese giant salamander looks as if its skin is at least three sizes too large.

All that wrinkled skin helps the Chinese giant salamander breathe. It's loaded with blood vessels that absorb oxygen from the fast-moving mountain streams where the salamander lives. Every so often, it swims up to the surface to gulp some air.

The giant salamander spends a lot of its time lurking in rock crevices in riverbanks, waiting for a fish, worm, or large insect to pass by. As soon as it spots a likely victim, the salamander snaps its mouth open, twists its head, and SWOOSH!—it sucks up its prey.

Giant salamanders are safe from most predators—but not from people! For centuries, people in China have eaten their meat and used other body parts to make medicine. Today, there are laws to protect these huge, ancient beasts.

39

Searching for Salamanders

Would you like to get to know salamanders better? Even though they live secret, silent lives, you can find them if you know where to look. You will need a field guide to amphibians, a notebook, a pen or pencil, and a hand lens that magnifies objects at least three times. If you're going to a pond, you may also want to take a large plastic tub, a net, and a sieve.

Begin your study of amphibians by looking for newt larvae. They have fringed gills and usually swim in the shallows. You may find adult newts resting just under the surface or hunting for prey near the shore. Watch the newts for a while and draw pictures of them in your notebook. Next to your pictures, write down what the salamanders are doing. To get a closer look, add some pond water to your tub and gently scoop the salamanders into the tub. What do you see? If

you float a leaf on the water, what do the salamanders do? Next, use the sieve to scoop up some water striders or whirligig beetles from the surface of the pond. Add them to the tub. What happens?

It's all right to pick up a newt, as long as you're careful. Wet your hands, then cup them under the animal. Gently lift your hands. Be sure to hold your hands just above the tub. You don't want this slippery creature to fall to the ground and get hurt! When you have studied the newts closely, tip the tub and let the water flow gently into the pond so the salamanders can swim free.

You probably won't see adult tiger salamanders or spotted salamanders. They live underground most of the year. But in early spring after a night of rain, you may find them laying eggs in a temporary pool. Even if you don't see the adults, you may be able to find clumps of their eggs stuck to underwater sticks. If you go back to the same

This spotted salamander has just finished laying her eggs.

Spotted salamander larvae

spot a few weeks later, you'll see the tiny larvae hunting for even tinier insects. By summer, the larvae will have grown up and gone, and the pool may dry up.

Luckily, there are other salamanders to look for in the summer. Go out into the woods, especially after a rain. If you look under rocks or in rotting stumps or logs, you may discover lungless salamanders— dusky, red-backed, four-toed, or slimy salamanders. Draw pictures of them in your notebook. Write down where you find them and what they are doing. Since most salamanders are active at night, they may not be doing much.

To see how the salamanders act at night, you can make a "guest house" for them and take them home. Put a layer of soil in a plastic jar or terrarium and cover it with wet leaves. Add some sticks and

This salamander is eating an earthworm.

rocks for the salamanders to hide under and some insects, such as small mealworms and crickets, for them to eat.

Watch the salamanders in the evening. Draw pictures of your guests and write down what you see. Do they eat the insects? What do they do when they meet each other? What else do you notice?

If you keep the salamanders for more than a day, keep the terrarium damp by misting it with a spray-bottle. After a few days, you should take your salamander guests back where you found them. Wild creatures need to be free!

Words to Know

amphibian—an animal that spends part of its life in water and part on land.

bog—a wetland area that is often covered with moss or other simple plants. When the plants die, they build up a layer called peat.

burrow—a shelter dug in the ground.

carnivore—an animal that eats the meat of other animals.

class—a group of creatures within a phylum that share certain characteristics.

eft—the land-living phase of a newt.

family—a group of creatures within an order that share certain characteristics.

genus (plural **genera**)—a group of creatures within a family that share certain characteristics.

gland—an organ in an animal's body that releases liquids. All salamanders have glands that secrete mucus. A few have glands that give off poisons.

habitat—the natural environment of an animal or plant.

hardwood forest—a forest with trees that lose their leaves each fall. Hardwood forests are often filled with oaks, maples, birches, hickories, aspens, and other trees.

kingdom—the largest group of biological classification.

larva (plural **larvae**)—the name for the young of some animals, including salamanders.

mammal—an animal with a backbone that has fur and feeds its young with mother's milk.

mucus—a slimy substance that covers the skin of a salamander and helps keep it moist.

order—a group of creatures within a class that share certain characteristics.

phylum (plural **phyla**)—a group of creatures within a kingdom that share certain characteristics.

predator—an animal that hunts other animals for food.

prey—an animal that's hunted for food.

reptile—an animal that lives on land, lays eggs, and is cold-blooded. Examples include alligators, turtles, snakes, and lizards.

species—a group of creatures within a genus that share certain characteristics. Members of a species can mate and produce young.

sphagnum—a type of moss. A moss is a simple plant that has no roots and must grow close to water.

Learning More

Books

Burns, Diane. *Take-Along Guide to Snakes, Salamanders, and Lizards.* Minocqua, WI: Northwood Press, 1995.

Conant, Roger. *Peterson's First Guide to Reptiles and Amphibians.* Boston: Houghton Mifflin, 1992.

Marsuka, Ed. *Salamanders.* New York: Child's World, 1996.

Smith, Hobart and Howard S. Zimm. *Golden Guide to Reptiles and Amphibians.* New York: Golden Press, 1987.

Winner, Cherie. *Salamanders.* Minneapolis, MN: Carolrhoda, 1993.

CD-ROM

Gunzi, Christiane. *Amphibians and Reptiles.* Integrated Communications.

Web Sites

Newt and Salamander
http://www.users.interport.net/~spiff/Newt%26Salamander.html
This site has information about keeping and caring for newts and salamanders and general information about and photos of these little, slimy creatures.

The Terrestrial Salamander Monitoring Program
http://www.users.interport.net/~spiff/Newt%26Salamander.html.
This site has information about the national effort to count land salamanders and keep track of their activities, so that we can learn more about them.

Index

About the Author

Sara Swan Miller has enjoyed working with children all her life, first as a nursery-school teacher, and later as an outdoor environmental educator at the Mohonk Preserve in New Paltz, New York. As the director of the Preserve school program, she has led hundreds of children on field trips and taught them the importance of appreciating and respecting the natural world.

She has written a number of children's books, including *Three Stories You Can Read to Your Dog*; *Three Stories You Can Read to Your Cat*; *What's in the Woods? An Outdoor Activity Book*; *Oh, Cats of Camp Rabbitbone!*; *Piggy in the Parlor and Other Tales*; *Better Than TV*; and *Will You Sting Me? Will You Bite? The Truth About Some Scary-Looking Insects*. She has also written many other books for the Animals in Order series.